WOMEN'S STORIES
from
HISTORY

STORIES OF THE STRUGGLE FOR THE VOTE

Votes for Women!

Charlotte Guillain

raintree
a Capstone company — publishers for children

Raintree is an imprint of Capstone Global Library Limited, a company incorporated in England and Wales having its registered office at 7 Pilgrim Street, London, EC4V 6LB – Registered company number: 6695582

www.raintree.co.uk
myorders@raintree.co.uk

Text © Capstone Global Library Limited 2015
The moral rights of the proprietor have been asserted.

Edited by Penny West
Designed by Philippa Jenkins
Original illustrations © Capstone Global Library Ltd 2015
Illustrated by Steve Noon - Advocate Art
Picture research by Tracy Cummins
Production by Helen McCreath
Originated by Capstone Global Library Ltd
Printed and bound in China by Leo Paper Group

ISBN 978 1 406 28947 3
18 17 16 15 14
10 9 8 7 6 5 4 3 2 1

British Library Cataloguing in Publication Data
A full catalogue record for this book is available from the British Library.

Acknowledgements
We would like to thank the following for permission to reproduce photographs and artwork: Capstone: Advocate Art/Steve Noon, 6, 19, 26, 40, 44, 52, 62, 73, 76, 91; Getty Images: The Print Collector, 4, Stock Montage, Cover; Thinkstock: Alex Wong, 94.

Every effort has been made to contact copyright holders of material reproduced in this book. Any omissions will be rectified in subsequent printings if notice is given to the publisher.

All the Internet addresses (URLs) given in this book were valid at the time of going to press. However, due to the dynamic nature of the Internet, some addresses may have changed, or sites may have changed or ceased to exist since publication. While the author and publisher regret any inconvenience this may cause readers, no responsibility for any such changes can be accepted by either the author or the publisher.

Contents

Introduction

Life for women around the world used to be very different from how it is for many women today. Most women had to obey the men in their lives and went from doing what their fathers told them to following what their husbands wanted.

When a woman married, her husband automatically owned all her property. Very few women worked, and usually those who did were desperate for money. These women often worked long hours in dreadful conditions and received very little pay in return. Very few women received a proper education and they had no rights. All the decisions in a woman's life were made by men.

By the 1850s, many women in different countries were starting to question this situation. They began joining together and asking for change.

Elizabeth Cady Stanton:
"You should have been a boy!"

Elizabeth Cady Stanton was one of the women who began questioning women's position in society. In the mid-1800s, she helped begin the struggle for women's right to vote. She is perhaps best remembered for helping organize the Seneca Falls Convention, where she presented a then-bold series of demands for women's rights. She continued this struggle throughout her long life, making Americans – and people around the world – reconsider women's rights and role in society.

Elizabeth was born in 1815 in Johnstown, New York. Her father was a lawyer and congressman. She was lucky to receive a good education, which was uncommon for girls at the time.

Elizabeth enjoyed talking to her father about the law. By studying the current laws affecting women, such as their loss of property to their husbands after marriage, young Elizabeth developed an early sense of injustice. Her passionate personality was already formed, as she later remembered:

So, when my attention was called to these [offensive] laws, I would mark them with a pencil, and I resolved to cut every one of them out of the books. However, this mutilation of my father's volumes was never accomplished, for the housekeeper warned him of what I proposed to do.

Elizabeth's family was traditional and strict in many ways. She was constantly looking for her father's approval and wanted to show him that she could achieve as much as her brothers. She later remembered:

I thought that the chief thing to be done in order to equal boys was to be learned and courageous. So I decided to study Greek and learn to manage a horse.

When she won a prize for Greek among a class of older boys, she described in her memoirs how she ran home to show her father, desperate for his recognition. But she was devastated by his reaction:

Then, while I stood looking and waiting for him to say something which would show that he recognized the equality of the daughter with the son, he kissed me on the forehead and exclaimed, with a sigh, "Ah, you should have been a boy!"

Moments of frustration and disappointment like this helped to shape Elizabeth into the young woman she became.

Members of Elizabeth's wider family were involved in the newly created abolitionist movement. There were 2.5 million slaves living and working in the United States in the late 1830s, usually existing in terrible conditions. The abolitionist movement was formed to stop this practice and to fight for the freedom and rights of all slaves.

It was at a relative's house that Elizabeth met Henry Stanton, an active abolitionist who often worked for no pay to fight for the cause he so passionately supported. Elizabeth and Henry fell in love and were married a year later. However, Elizabeth had the minister remove the vow to "obey" from her wedding vows, saying, "I obstinately refused to obey one with whom I supposed I was entering into an equal relation".

After their wedding in 1840, they travelled to the United Kingdom, where Henry was attending the World's Anti-Slavery Convention. On arrival, both Elizabeth and another American woman, Lucretia Mott, found that they were not allowed into the convention because they were women!

They fought hard against this restriction, gaining support from many male delegates. They were eventually allowed to enter, but only if they sat behind a curtain where the men could not see them. This treatment made Elizabeth feel very angry and humiliated and led her to think more and more about women's rights.

In the early years of her marriage, Elizabeth spent some time in Boston, where she got to know other like-minded women and men. Together, they would discuss the need for change and the ways that they could persuade others and obtain rights for both slaves and women. Elizabeth's outgoing personality and wit made her a popular guest in the forward-thinking circles of Boston.

By 1847, Elizabeth and Henry had three children (they would eventually have seven), and they moved to Seneca Falls, New York. Elizabeth was a warm and supportive mother, and she made sure her daughters had the same opportunities as her sons. Later, her two daughters would both attend universities.

But, unlike in Boston, Elizabeth missed the company of like-minded adults.

She later wrote of this time:

In Seneca Falls, my life was comparatively solitary, and the change from Boston was somewhat depressing...

I suffered with mental hunger, which, like an empty stomach, is very depressing. I had books, but no stimulating companionship... I now fully understood the practical difficulties most women had to contend with in the isolated household, and the impossibility of woman's best development if in contact, the chief part of her life, with servants and children...

In this tempest-tossed condition of mind I received an invitation to spend the day with Lucretia Mott [the social reformer she had first met in London]. I poured out, that day, the torrent of my long-accumulating discontent... We decided, then and there, to call a "Woman's Rights Convention".

The Seneca Falls Convention, as it became known, was held in 1848. Elizabeth organized the two-day meeting about women's rights with several other local women. More than 300 people attended, including Mott and Frederick Douglass, the African American writer and campaigner, who spoke in support of women's rights.

Elizabeth spoke to the convention and read a document she had written called "The Declaration of Sentiments", which was based on the US Declaration of Independence. This document outlined the various ways in which women were denied their rights. It particularly focused on how wrong it was for a woman to lose her identity, property and rights when she married.

Elizabeth wrote:

We are assembled ... to declare our right to be free as man is free, to be represented in the government which we are taxed to support, to have such disgraceful laws as give man the power to chastise and imprison his wife, to take the wages which she earns, the property which she inherits, and, in case of separation, the children of her love...

The Declaration of Sentiments called for women's rights to be recognized by the law and it declared that those rights should include the vote. Elizabeth declared:

all men and women are created equal, that they are endowed by their creator with certain unalienable rights, that among these are life, liberty, and the pursuit of happiness.

Next, Elizabeth began campaigning for women's rights as parents. At that time, if a married couple divorced, the father automatically got custody of the children, and they would live with him rather than with their mother. This law made it very hard for women who wanted to escape unhappy marriages but could not accept losing their children.

Elizabeth also began fighting for women's property rights and for their employment and income rights. She campaigned for a bill that was passed successfully, granting married women in New York their own property rights. Their husbands would no longer automatically own all their property when they married. These were some of the same laws that she had vowed to change as a girl.

By 1850, women's rights conventions were taking place across the United States and Elizabeth was seen as a leader of this movement. She wrote articles for magazines and journals and had letters and speeches published all over the country to gather support. She managed to juggle her family life with her busy work schedule, often writing after the children went to bed. Her energetic personality helped her manage, and she enjoyed the challenge, saying, "I am always busy, which is perhaps the chief reason why I am always well".

An important moment in Elizabeth's life came in 1851, when she met another well-known campaigner for women's rights, Susan B. Anthony. The two women became fast friends, despite their different personalities.

Elizabeth was warm and social. In contrast, Susan – at least to strangers – seemed a bit more reserved and serious. But they made a formidable team as they planned campaigns and made speeches at gatherings and conventions. Elizabeth (opposite, on the right) was especially good at writing in a persuasive way and giving powerful speeches. Susan (opposite, on the left) was skilled in organizing people and gathering support. Elizabeth wrote about their friendship and collaboration as follows:

> In thought and sympathy we were one,
> and in the division of labor we exactly
> complemented each other... Together, we have
> made arguments that have stood unshaken
> through the storms of long years; arguments
> that no one has answered.

In 1854, Elizabeth was invited to speak to the New York legislature, where she argued for change. She and Susan put pressure on the nation's decision-makers for years, demanding that they make changes to the law in favour of women's rights.

Often they were mocked and ridiculed by the lawmakers they were addressing, the general public or the press. Many men, and also many women, believed that women should not be allowed to speak in public or express their opinions.

Once a group of women asked Elizabeth how she could behave in such an immodest way, by putting herself in the public eye. They argued that as a woman she should stay private and keep quiet.

Her response was to point out that speaking at meetings and conventions was no more public than dancing at a ball, which she had seen all of them doing the night before!

Despite this widespread lack of support, Elizabeth's persistence, her belief that she was right and her solid arguments helped lead to a law being passed in 1860. This law gave married women the right to earn their own wages and have equal custody of their children. It was a huge victory that made women's lives more bearable.

The American Civil War began in 1861, putting a stop to Elizabeth's work fighting for women's rights. Instead she switched her energies into campaigning for the North and the abolition of slavery. She wrote about how the work of women was just as important as that of men in fighting the war:

> While he buckled on his knapsack and marched forth, she planned the campaigns which brought the nation victory; fought in the ranks, when she could do so without detection; inspired the sanitary commission; gathered needed supplies for the army; provided nurses for the hospitals; comforted the sick; smoothed the pillows of the dying; inscribed the last messages of love to those far away; and marked the resting places where the brave men fell.

Elizabeth set up the Women's Loyal National League with Susan B. Anthony, to pressure the US government into abolishing slavery. They organized a petition and gathered around 400,000 signatures in support of their cause. In 1865, with the Civil War ended, the 13th Amendment was finally added to the Constitution and slavery was abolished in the United States.

However, Elizabeth and many other campaigners for women's right to vote became frustrated as more people began to support the right of black men to vote. Elizabeth refused to support the vote for black men only, instead demanding that this right should be extended to black and white women, too.

She must have felt very torn by this decision, having campaigned so hard to abolish slavery and fought for the rights of slaves to be equal citizens. Many people criticized her for fighting against the 14th and 15th Amendments, which focused on the rights of black men.

However, Elizabeth knew that she had to stick to her principles and keep arguing for women's suffrage. She quickly turned her energies back into the fight for women's rights.

Elizabeth became the co-editor of a weekly newspaper about women's rights, called *The Revolution*. The slogan on the front page of the newspaper was: "Men, their rights and nothing more; women, their rights and nothing less." The newspaper, and Elizabeth's powerfully written articles, had a huge influence on the spread of interest in women's rights in the country.

Elizabeth also began an exhausting tour of the United States with Susan B. Anthony, speaking at meetings and gatherings about the need for women's suffrage. She was involved in establishing the National Woman Suffrage Association (NWSA) and fought for an amendment to the Constitution that would give the vote to all, men and women.

Other women who had campaigned alongside Elizabeth for women's rights disagreed with Elizabeth's position, believing that black men should be given the vote first. The women who disagreed formed the American Woman Suffrage Association (AWSA).

Elizabeth and the other members of the NWSA became known as the more radical group, with its members taking more direct action to highlight their arguments. They called for equal rights for women in employment and education and wanted immediate voting rights for women.

Elizabeth spent eight years working tirelessly to bring more women to the cause, persuading them to sign a petition asking Congress for a 16th Amendment, which would give women the vote. This amendment was introduced in 1878 but it was voted down in 1886.

Both groups began to make an impact and recognized the importance of each other. In 1890, they joined together to form the National American Woman Suffrage Association (NAWSA). Elizabeth was the first president of this united organization.

She also continued to write books and articles, and gave speeches every year, despite her advancing age. She had worked hard all her life to fight for change and improve women's lives. Now she was ready to hand over to the next generation of campaigners to finally win the vote for all American women.

Susan B. Anthony:
Arrested for voting

Joining Elizabeth Cady Stanton in the fight for women's suffrage was her dear friend, Susan B. Anthony, who became a public face of the campaign for women's rights. Susan dedicated her life to the cause, tirelessly touring, speaking and writing until she died at age 86.

Susan was born in Massachusetts in 1820 and had an unusual upbringing for the time. Her close family members were Quakers, a religious group which believed women were equal to men. She grew up surrounded by people who felt it was their duty to take an active role in helping to fight injustice in society.

Susan was an unusually bright child, learning to read and write at age three. When she was six, her family moved to New York. She followed her family's fight against injustice when, at age 16, she collected petitions against slavery.

For a time, when her father's business was doing well, she was sent to a good Quaker boarding school. Unfortunately, in 1837, much of the United States suffered from an economic crisis and many people lost their jobs and businesses. Susan's father lost his livelihood and the family home.

As a result, at 17, Susan had to leave her school and go to work as a teacher to help support the family. She was an excellent teacher and became a senior member of staff at her school. During this time, she got to know families who were struggling with poverty. Her kind, patient demeanour made her a good listener, and she grew to understand how hard life could be for women in this situation.

Meanwhile, her family had moved to a farm and they became involved in the abolitionist movement. Important meetings were held at their farm, with well-known campaigners such as Frederick Douglass coming to speak there.

Susan also started to meet people who were discussing women's rights, such as Amy Post, who attended the Seneca Falls Convention in 1848. Susan could see that many people now accepted that women should have equal rights to men.

Susan joined a women's temperance society, which campaigned to stop people drinking too much alcohol. It was a cause she felt strongly about, having seen how alcohol could destroy families.

However, she felt frustrated that women in the temperance movement were kept separate from men and were treated as less important. Women were not allowed to speak at a men's temperance meeting, but they were told they could "listen and learn".

In 1851, Susan met Elizabeth Cady Stanton for the first time. While Susan had been focusing on how the temperance movement could improve women's lives, Elizabeth had been campaigning to get the law changed to give women more rights. When the two women met, they began to share their ideas and became a united force. They quickly became very close friends as well as colleagues.

Together, they were an amazing team.

Elizabeth described their partnership as "I forged the thunderbolts and she fired them". In turn, Susan claimed "Mrs Stanton is my sentence maker, my pen artist".

Their different temperaments also complemented each other, as the focused Susan sometimes made the more social Elizabeth stay in and finish a speech or essay. They also merged their different lifestyles. Elizabeth was a wife and a mother to, eventually, seven children, while Susan never married or had children. Over the years, Susan would help watch Elizabeth's children when Elizabeth needed to get work done. Often she would travel to Elizabeth's house in the evening, when her friend's children were asleep, and they would talk and plan late into the night.

Susan and Elizabeth first worked together to set up the Women's New York State Temperance Society, which they declared was of equal importance to the men's temperance society.

They demanded that a woman should have the right to divorce a husband who drank too much alcohol, without suffering the terrible consequence of losing the custody of her children or her belongings and income.

Now Susan was ready to devote her energy to fighting for women's right to vote. She saw this as the only way women could truly have any chance of making changes in society. She also saw it as their basic right, saying:

> It was we, the people, not we, the white male citizens, nor yet we, the male citizens; but we, the whole people, who formed this Union.

It took courage for Susan and her friends to speak up for women's rights. They were often named and ridiculed in newspapers when they spoke or campaigned in public. Susan became known for her calm bravery as she faced one hostile crowd after another, always managing to keep her composure. She knew she could not bring about change without taking these risks. As she once said:

> Cautious, careful people, always casting about to preserve their reputations ... can never effect a reform.

Susan set up the New York State Woman's Rights Committee with Elizabeth and this group worked hard to argue that laws should be changed in support of women. As well as demanding the vote for women, they asked that the laws regarding married women's property, women's employment and the custody of their children should be changed.

Susan was especially good at organizing people and campaigns. She was skilled in having a strategic overview of a campaign and had plenty of energy to organize supporters so that their protests and demands would have a significant impact.

She made sure that well-known speakers arrived to speak to crowds of supporters just before politicians were due to discuss changes to the law. This got the attention of the newspapers and the lawmakers themselves.

As she became busier and busier with the cause, Susan's lifestyle allowed her to be fully focused on the cause of suffrage and women's rights. She was a single woman who could support herself and go wherever she was needed at any time. Indeed, she lived by her own motto:

I think the girl who is able to earn her own living and pay her own way should be as happy as anybody on earth. The sense of independence and security is very sweet.

Susan's energy was vital, as she spent a lot of time travelling around the country. Travel was not easy at that time, especially in winter when snow could block train tracks and roads.

Susan described one perilous journey in a letter to her family (see page 26):

Just emerged from a long line of snowdrifts and stopped at this little country tavern, supped and am now roasting over a hot stove. Oh, oh, what an experience! No trains running and we have had a thirty-six mile ride in a sleigh. Once we seemed lost in a drift full fifteen feet deep. The driver went on ahead to a house, and there we sat shivering. When he returned we found he had gone over a fence into a field, so we had to dismount and plough through the snow after the sleigh; then we reseated ourselves, but oh, the poor horses!

Susan was so effective at mobilizing support across the nation that the Anti-Slavery Society also asked her to be their main agent in New York. During the American Civil War,

Susan concentrated on the abolition of slavery.

Her father died in 1862, leaving Susan and her brothers and sisters full of grief. He had always supported her arguments for women's rights and losing him was a great blow to her. It took her some time to recover, but a year later she turned back to her work. She spent 18 months writing letters, gathering support and getting signatures from all over the country for a petition to abolish slavery.

Susan spent several months in Kansas with her brother Daniel, writing about a variety of topics for his newspaper. She was there when the 13th Amendment to the Constitution abolished slavery in the United States.

Now people began discussing what rights freed slaves should have as citizens. When the issue of voting came up, many people argued that black males should be given the right to vote, but they did not extend this right to women of any colour.

These proposed changes to the Constitution were supposed to help rebuild the country after the Civil War, but Susan and her colleagues strongly believed that the changes would be incomplete without giving women the right to vote, too.

By the end of 1865, she was back in the eastern United States, ready to help launch the first national campaign for women's suffrage. She helped to found the American Equal Rights Association, which demanded that people of both sexes should have the same rights. In 1868, Susan and Elizabeth set up a newspaper, *The Revolution*.

When campaigners for women's right

to vote split in 1869, Susan stayed with Elizabeth and helped to set up the National Woman Suffrage Association (NWSA). They used the 14th and 15th Amendments to the Constitution to make their arguments.

The 14th Amendment had given every citizen of the United States the same protection under the law. The 15th Amendment gave all men the right to vote, regardless of their race.

Susan and Elizabeth began to argue that these amendments had actually granted women the right to vote. They pointed out that the changes to the law had linked the right to vote with citizenship, and surely women were citizens?

More politicians and newspapers were starting to be swayed by these arguments.

After Susan made a speech in Dayton, Ohio, the *Dayton Herald* declared:

> She made a clear, logical and lawyerlike argument, in sprightly language, that women being persons are citizens, and as citizens, voters. We think that none who examine her authorities and line of discussion can avoid her conclusions, and we are certain that many of the ablest jurists of the land have the honor (logically and legally) to coincide with her argument.

Supporters of the NWSA, the organization led by Susan and Elizabeth, started to take direct action. This included women trying to place their vote in elections. Susan tried this herself in 1872. With two of her sisters and a group of friends, she was successfully registered to vote and attempted to cast her ballot on Election Day. She was arrested about two weeks later.

She was supported at her trial by her local newspaper, the *Rochester Express*:

> Miss Anthony had a loftier end in view than the making of a sensation when she registered her name and cast her vote. The act was in harmony with a life steadily consecrated to a high purpose from which she has never wavered... There is at least one woman in the land – and we believe there are a good many more – who does not whine others into helping her over a hard spot, or even plead for help, but bravely helps herself and puts her hand to the plough without turning back.

By 1878, Susan was again gathering support for a proposed amendment to the Constitution to allow women to vote, but it was 1886 before the proposal reached the Senate. To Susan's frustration, after all those years of hard work, the proposal was defeated. She and her friends seemed to be fighting against the tide.

However, Susan herself was becoming well known across the United States as she continued to travel from city to city, making speeches and organizing supporters. Many local newspapers showed interest in what she had to say, and other women's groups across the nation joined forces with her with the aim of improving women's rights. Now in her sixties, she became a celebrity and the face of women's suffrage.

When the NWSA and the American Woman

Suffrage Association (AWSA) merged in 1890, Elizabeth Cady Stanton became the first president of the united organization. Susan took over two years later. By now she was in her seventies.

The cause was given a boost the following year, when New Zealand gave its female citizens suffrage and some states in the United States, such as Colorado, started to give women the vote. Susan continued to travel, spending time in many different states and abroad right up until her death in 1906, four years after her friend Elizabeth died. Towards the end of her life, Susan reflected:

> Oh, if I could but live another century and see the fruition of all the work for women! There is so much yet to be done.

Clementina Black:
Giving the poor a voice

In the mid-1850s, life for British women was very similar to that of women in the United States. Women were expected to be obedient to their fathers, brothers and husbands, and their education was not considered important. A woman's role was to do as she was told and look after the family. But a woman called Clementina Black challenged these expectations, as she became a powerful voice in the fight for women's rights in the workplace and their right to vote. Her work set the stage for the next generation of women's rights advocates.

Born in 1853 in Brighton, England, Clementina was educated at home by her own mother, who taught her to speak German and French. Her brothers also helped to educate Clementina and her sisters. She loved to read both classical literature and popular contemporary books.

Sadly, her mother died when Clementina was just a young woman and she suddenly found herself expected to care for her sick father and younger brothers and sisters. Clementina was not willing to accept a domestic role for the rest of her life. She took her commitment to care for her family very seriously, but she loved learning and particularly wanted to be a writer.

Somehow she managed to find time to write short stories around keeping house and her job as a teacher, which was needed to bring money into the household. In 1875, she had her first short story published in a magazine. Clementina then went on to write longer novels, including *A Sussex Idyll*.

When her siblings were older and able to look after themselves, Clementina moved to London to start an independent life. She lived in the city with her sisters, Emma and Grace, and was able to devote more time to her writing. She spent hours studying and researching in the British Museum. She also started to become more and more interested in the problems she saw in society around her, particularly for working women.

Clementina began to meet other people in London who were campaigning for change. Through these new friends she became involved with an organization called the Women's Protective and Provident League (WPPL).

This group aimed to give help to poorer workers when they retired and needed medical help or support. Many ordinary people had very little income when they became too old to work and it was a struggle for many elderly people to survive. A lot of workers also suffered from injuries or illnesses that had been caused by the difficult work they had done all their lives. Clementina's work with the WPPL to help these people was a lifeline.

Through her work, Clementina discovered that women who did the same work as men were paid less. She found this very unfair and began to argue that they deserved equal pay.

She spent a lot of time talking to workers and collecting evidence to show that there were great economic injustices for women who were working just as hard as men. As she said:

> Surely the time was coming when the law, which was the representative of the organized will of the people, would declare that British workers should no longer work for less than they could live upon.

In 1886, Clementina became honorary secretary of the WPPL, which later changed its name to the Women's Trade Union League. In the same year, there were riots in London as the city's poor protested in the streets. They were angry about widespread unemployment and the economic hardships in their lives. The rioting shocked many wealthier Londoners, who had never been confronted by poverty before. Clementina felt strongly that such poverty needed to be addressed and people's lives improved to benefit all of society.

She began travelling around the country talking to working women, trying to persuade them to join a trade union, which would help them to fight for their rights. A trade union is an organization of workers who do a similar job, who can stand together to protect and improve their rights more effectively than they could as individuals.

Clementina wanted to give poor, working women the support of more educated middle-class women and the stronger working men's trade unions. This support would help them achieve change and improve their lives. At the Trades Union Congress, a big meeting of all trade unions in the United Kingdom, she argued that women should receive equal pay.

Clementina was also involved in the

Consumers' League, which tried to persuade the public to avoid companies that paid women low wages.

For example, she helped to organize a campaign that encouraged customers to boycott Bryant and May matches because of the working conditions in their factory. She wanted people to buy products from other companies so that Bryant and May would realize they had to improve conditions to stay in business. To help organize a strike at the Bryant and May factory, Clementina joined forces with another campaigner for women's rights, Annie Besant.

The women who worked in the factory were known as match girls and they worked in terrible conditions. Their working day could be as long as 14 hours, but they were paid very little and their health was affected by the chemicals that were used in making the matches. They were even fined by their employer if they missed a day's work, so it was very hard for them to make a living.

When word spread that Clementina and Annie were talking to the workers about fighting for their rights, the owners of the factory tried to force the match girls to sign a document that declared they were happy with their conditions. However, when one woman was sacked for refusing to sign the paper, all 1,400 match girls stood together and went on strike.

Clementina and Annie supported these working women by raising donations to help them survive while they were not being paid. They also helped to negotiate better conditions with the management of the factory and end the strike.

In 1890, Clementina started fighting a new battle for working women. She put forward the idea that all employees should only have to work a limited number of hours. She also argued that all workers should have rest breaks built into their working day.

Many women who worked for manufacturers at that time did the work in their own homes. For example, a lot of women in London worked at home sewing clothes for large tailoring companies. Clementina made sure that her arguments for workers' rights included these women.

She persuaded the London City Council to make sure that all companies in London followed new rules to ensure all workers' welfare. Still, Clementina became more and more convinced that not enough was being done to help the poorer women in society.

She became one of the founding members of the Women's Trade Union Association, which became the Women's Industrial Council (WIC) a few years later. Many of the WIC's members were well-educated middle-class women like Clementina. They were able to observe the lives of working women and write detailed reports calling for change. Using the evidence they collected, they were able to persuade more members of the public to support their cause and to convince government that laws needed to be changed.

Clementina became editor of the WIC's journal and she later became president of the WIC. She was focused on helping poorer working women and devoted her time to writing articles highlighting their plight. She also spent a lot of time making speeches around the country, arguing that women deserved equal pay to men.

Clementina was described as follows by a colleague:

> While her brightness, ready sympathy, and complete absence of self-assertion make her popular ... only those who have worked with her ... can fully appreciate her untiring industry, her tact and patience, and above all, her unvarying good temper under the most aggravating circumstances.

When her brother and his wife died, Clementina began looking after her young niece. When her father died a year later, he left her £1,000 (around $1,700). This was a lot of money in those days. Although it was hard for Clementina to deal with the loss of these close family members, the money her father gave her helped Clementina to care for her niece.

In 1896, Clementina launched a campaign for a legal minimum wage. She was particularly interested in women who earned money working from home, especially those involved in the tailoring industry who would sew for long hours in bad light for very little money. Women who worked in this way in the East End of London were described as working in "sweatshops". In Clementina's book, *Sweated Industry and the Minimum Wage,* she described what life was like for many of these women:

> Ill-health, indeed, is the chronic state of the woman home worker. She misses that regular daily journey to and from her work-place which ensures to the factory worker at least a daily modicum of air and exercise... If she depends upon her own exertions she will inevitably be ill fed and ill clothed ... the woman who is self-supported often earns less, even at the same rates of pay, than the woman who is comfortably married. The half-starved and apathetic human creature cannot maintain a high output of work... Her work grows, like herself, poorer and poorer; and the employer thereupon declares that it is worth no more than its poor price.

Clementina made sure she had done a lot of research before writing the book, which showed many examples of poor working conditions for women, men and children employed in a range of different industries. These ranged from making paper bags to filling pots of jam.

She took care to point out to wealthier readers that many of the things they needed in their everyday lives were produced by these workers, who suffered as a result. Even the production of expensive, high-quality goods often involved the mistreatment of many poor workers.

Clementina went on to argue the case for a minimum wage, giving examples of where this had been a success elsewhere in the world. She wanted to persuade readers that it would improve all of society if these workers were taken out of poverty. She believed that only changes to the law could help improve the working and living conditions for thousands of women, and she felt strongly that women should be among the people making and changing the laws.

As time passed and the situation for women in society improved very little, Clementina and many other people began to see the importance of women winning the right to vote. She drew up a document called the "Suffrage Declaration", which called for women's right to suffrage, or the vote. This was signed by 257,000 women in the United Kingdom.

Clementina went on to become the honorary secretary of the Women's Franchise Declaration Committee, an organization that was devoted to campaigning for women's right to vote. She spoke at meetings all around the country where women were starting to discuss the need for suffrage. She was one of a group of women who went to speak to Prime Minister Herbert Asquith to try and persuade him of the need to change the law and involve women in elections.

In 1915, Clementina had another book published: *Married Women's Work*. At that time, most women who worked would stop their employment after marriage. They were expected to focus instead on the home and bringing up a family.

In her book, Clementina argued that work was good for women's independence and self-respect. She showed how women could help each other manage the responsibilities of their lives by working cooperatively.

During World War I (1914–1918), many

women began working to help with the war effort. Many people, both men and women, recognized the importance of this contribution and changed their attitudes to women's place in society.

However, a large number of men and women still believed that women belonged in the home, despite the vital role they had played in the war years. Clementina complained about this attitude in an article. She wrote that a great national asset was being wasted because women were not being given opportunities.

Clementina's work and writing had helped to lay the ground for other campaigners for women's rights, who were ready to give their lives for the right to vote.

Carrie Chapman Catt:
"The woman's hour has struck"

Just a few years after Clementina Black was born in the United Kingdom, another future leader of the women's movement was born in the United States: Carrie Chapman Catt. Working with Susan B. Anthony and other leaders in the suffrage movement, she continued where older leaders left off and helped make the long-awaited 19th Amendment a reality.

Carrie Clinton Lane was born in Wisconsin in 1859 and moved to Iowa when she was seven. She noticed at an early age how unfair life was for women. At age 13, she felt outraged when she discovered her mother was not allowed to vote in the presidential election, but her father was.

Her parents were farmers and held the very traditional views of the time. Her father did not want her to go to university and refused to support her, so Carrie taught at a school to save the money she would need to go to university. She paid her own way through her studies by washing dishes and working in the library.

While she was a student, Carrie got involved in public speaking, which was very unusual for female students at the time. She even organized a debate on women's right to vote, long before many of her fellow students had even started to consider the issue. Carrie was both the valedictorian (top student) and the only woman in her graduating class at Iowa State.

Carrie went on to study law. Then, she became a teacher and was the first female superintendent of schools in her district. These roles helped her to become a very good leader and organizer of people.

In 1885, Carrie married Leo Chapman, the editor of a newspaper. After their marriage, Carrie began working with him and soon became co-editor of the newspaper. She introduced a new section to the newspaper called "Woman's World". This gave her the opportunity to spread her ideas about women's rights to a wide readership.

Then she joined the Iowa Woman Suffrage Association, starting to get involved in the debate about women's rights at a national level.

Sadly, her husband Leo died just a few years after they married and so Carrie worked alone as a reporter and a lecturer to support herself. She was keen to find other women who also wanted to win the vote and decided to make this the focus of her work.

She became a leader of her local campaigning organization, the Iowa Woman Suffrage Association, in 1889. The following year, Carrie married George Catt, a wealthy engineer who supported Carrie's views. He agreed that she could spend several months each year campaigning all over the country for women's right to vote.

George sometimes spoke in support of women's suffrage at meetings himself and his financial backing made it much easier for Carrie to fight for her beliefs. She said, "We made a team to work for the cause."

Carrie was very good at organizing

campaigns and rallies, but initially she felt frustrated that she did not seem to be able to make any impact.

She travelled to South Dakota to try and win supporters, but she felt that some male politicians were trying to block suffrage campaigners from making any progress. She realized that a lot of work needed to be done to educate the general public and show them the importance of the vote for women and for society in general.

She summed up her frustration – and showed her keen wit – when she said:

> There are whole precincts of voters in this country whose united intelligence does not equal that of one representative American woman.

In 1892, Carrie and George had moved to New York and Carrie became even more involved in national campaigning, in particular for the National American Woman Suffrage Association (NAWSA).

Her great organizational skills were vital in gathering more support for the NAWSA and she helped to set up and improve many local branches of the organization around the country. She also devoted a lot of her time to giving speeches at meetings and conventions.

The NAWSA held a national convention in the same year and Susan B. Anthony, who was president of the organization, set up a new committee led by Carrie. Susan B. Anthony was aware that she needed to pass on her role as leader to younger women, and Carrie was one whom she singled out. Carrie's spirited determination and skill as a commanding speaker made her a strong candidate.

Carrie's new role on the committee involved setting up a network of women around the country. This network would organize meetings and educate other women to gain more supporters for the fight for women's suffrage. She had to raise funds, find people to speak and organize their trips, venues for speeches and accommodation. She also had to provide support for new local suffrage groups so they could grow and develop real influence.

Carrie did such a good job that in 1900 she became president of NAWSA. She continued to work hard, training other women to take direct action to highlight their cause. She organized the International Woman's

Suffrage Association to coordinate women's efforts around the world. She was impatient for change, once saying:

In the adjustment of the new order of things, we women demand an equal voice; we shall accept nothing less.

In 1904, Carrie had to stop her work to care for her sick husband. He died a year later. Shortly afterwards, Susan B. Anthony, Carrie's brother and her mother also died. These losses were very hard, and she was advised to take some time to recover and regain her energy.

In the following years, she travelled to many different countries, talking to women with similar ideas and promoting the need for women's suffrage internationally. Carrie was very good at unifying different groups within the movement who held opposing views, and she could usually help them to find a compromise and move on together.

In 1915, Carrie returned to the United States from her travels and became president of NAWSA again. The organization had become divided, with different members arguing for different ways forward. Carrie disagreed with activists such as Alice Paul who wanted the Constitution to be amended so all women in the United States could vote.

Carrie had a different idea. She belonged to a group that proposed the best approach would be to target one state at a time and fight for the vote in each state before moving on to the next. When this gradual change started to happen, Carrie argued that there would be a much better case for a constitutional amendment. She launched this campaign, which she called a "Winning Plan". Some of the states in the western United States were beginning to give women the vote, but other states in the East and South were resisting this change.

Some people left the NAWSA because of her views, but she was determined to see her strategy through.

Carrie made a speech in New York, saying:

in the name of the women of today who ...
have no voice in the regulation of the conditions
under which they work; in the name of the
1,000,000 women dedicated in clubs that
are working for the uplift of humanity; in the
name of the mothers who must send their
children out into a world over which they
have no control, we appeal to you. Justice gave
you the vote. In the name of that same great
virtue, we ask you to give it to us.

More influential states started to grant women the vote, such as New York in 1917.

Carrie's cause was greatly boosted by President Woodrow Wilson showing his support for a constitutional amendment. Her goal was finally in sight! Carrie and her colleagues worked hard campaigning and lobbying all over the country to gain further support.

She made a speech before Congress, declaring:

> The time for woman suffrage has come. The woman's hour has struck. If parties prefer to postpone action longer and thus do battle with this idea, they challenge the inevitable. The idea will not perish; the party which opposes it may... Woman suffrage is coming — you know it. Will you, Honorable Senators and Members of the House of Representatives, help or hinder it?

On 26 August 1920, Tennessee became the 36th and final state needed to pass the 19th Amendment. Finally women in the United States had won the vote. Carrie reflected on how it had taken 52 years of work by three generations of the women's movement to achieve this. She recognized the importance of what was achieved when she said:

74

The vote is the emblem of your equality, women of America, the guarantee of your liberty.

However, once the vote was won, Carrie did not sit back and rest! She helped to establish the League of Women Voters. This organization was set up to help women exercise their new right to vote in an informed way. Once the League was up and running, Carrie moved her attention away from women's rights and concentrated on working for peace in a world that had been devastated by World War I.

She firmly believed that women who could vote would be able to influence world politics in a positive way and help avoid future wars. She organized a conference for peace in 1925 and continued to work for this goal until the end of her life.

Emmeline Pankhurst:
Leader of the suffragettes

While Carrie Chapman Catt was helping women in the United States win the vote state by state, women in the United Kingdom were struggling to make their voices heard.

British campaigners for women's suffrage had always tended to use peaceful forms of protest. They had tried to win sympathy with the public and in Parliament but they were making no ground.

As a result, in 1903, a woman named Emmeline Pankhurst founded a new group called the Women's Social and Political Union (WSPU). She planned to make sure that the cause was finally noticed.

Emmeline was born in 1858 and grew up in

Manchester in a family of activists. Emmeline was a very bright child. Her parents supported the anti-slavery campaign in the United States when she was young, and so she became aware of the need to fight injustice from an early age.

Emmeline's mother was involved in campaigning for women's rights and she took her daughter to her first women's suffrage meeting when Emmeline was 16. Emmeline wrote in her autobiography that:

> I had always been an unconscious suffragist. With my temperament and my surroundings I could scarcely have been otherwise.

She also became interested in politics after reading the newspapers aloud to her father. Despite the fact that she was clever and interested in learning, her early education was not as good as that of her brothers. She later wrote of a similar experience to Elizabeth Cady Stanton, when her father came to kiss her goodnight and said, "What a pity she wasn't born a lad!"

However, at the age of 15, Emmeline was lucky enough to be sent to study in Paris at one of the best schools for girls in Europe. She was able to learn subjects such as chemistry that were not generally studied by girls at that time. She also made many life-long friends in France.

Emmeline married a lawyer called Richard Pankhurst. He was an activist who supported women's rights, and he wrote the bill to grant married women the right to keep their own property and be guardians of their children. This proposal resulted in a change to the law.

Emmeline and Richard had five children over the course of 10 years. Emmeline felt strongly that she could be both a mother and an activist, and she hired servants at home to help her balance these pursuits. Her two eldest daughters, Christabel and Sylvia, would grow up to become active members of the women's movement. As her own parents had done for her, Emmeline created an environment full of political passion for her family.

Emmeline formed an organization called the Women's Franchise League and held the first meeting in her London home. The main aim of this group was to argue for married women to be able to vote in local elections. Emmeline was very determined to fight for the rights of both women and the poor.

She returned to live in Manchester in 1893

and during the following year she drove to a market in the city at 6 a.m. every day to get donations of food to hand out to unemployed families. At that time, there was very little help for people who found themselves in extreme poverty. Many families ended up in workhouses. These were places where desperately poor people received lodgings and basic food in return for long, hard days of labour. Emmeline described a visit to one workhouse in Manchester:

> The first time I went into the place I was horrified to see little girls seven and eight years old on their knees scrubbing the cold stones of the long corridors. These little girls were clad, summer and winter, in thin cotton frocks, low in the neck and short sleeved. At night they wore nothing at all, night dresses being considered too good for paupers.

She also met many old women in workhouses who were ending their days in poverty. These women had not been able to save to support themselves in their old age because all their income had gone into bringing up a family. Emmeline felt angry that these elderly women had to end their lives in such hardship and poverty. She was sure that giving women the right to vote would help to take them out of such awful circumstances. She said:

> You must make women count as much as men; you must have an equal standard of morals; and the only way to enforce that is through giving women political power so that you can get that equal moral standard registered in the laws of the country. It is the only way.

In the same year, her dedicated campaigning resulted in women winning the right to take part in local elections. But women still were not able to vote in general elections, which appointed Members of Parliament (MPs) to represent them in Parliament.

Then Emmeline's husband died and she was left as a single parent. She had very little income and growing children to support. Emmeline had to find a paid job, and worked as registrar of births and deaths in a poor district of Manchester. She said of this role that:

> I was shocked to be reminded over and over again of the little respect there was in the world for women and children.

By 1903, Emmeline realized that the peaceful campaigning she had taken part in was having no effect on changing the laws regarding women's rights. She was a member of the National Union of Women's Suffrage Societies (NUWSS), which disagreed with her increasingly radical ideas. Emmeline set up the Women's Social and Political Union (WSPU) because of these differences. Unlike the NUWSS, which had male members, the WSPU was only for women. Moreover, she said, "'Deeds, not words' was to be our permanent motto."

Susan B. Anthony visited Manchester around this time and her speeches made a strong impression on Emmeline and her daughters. Emmeline set up the WSPU with the aim of taking whatever steps were necessary to win the vote for women.

Emmeline and the WSPU started out working in familiar ways, organizing public meetings and rallies and sending petitions to Parliament. But Emmeline and other WSPU members soon felt that they were not being taken seriously and their members were being denied opportunities to speak in public. So, Emmeline began to shift the strategy of the WSPU in a more radical direction.

Direct action involved protestors chaining themselves to railings so they could shout their message in the street without being removed. They also wrote slogans in public places and caused damage to buildings, such as smashing windows. All three of Emmeline's daughters – Christabel, Sylvia and Adela – joined their mother's fight and made headlines for being arrested for public protests. Emmeline justified such actions when she said:

> You have to make more noise than anybody else, you have to make yourself more obtrusive than anybody else, you have to fill all the papers more than anybody else, in fact you have to be there all the time and see that they do not snow you under, if you are really going to get your reform realized.

In the United Kingdom, campaigners who took more direct action to get results became known as "suffragettes".

Many people at the time felt that Emmeline's approach to campaigning had a negative effect. The actions of the WSPU campaigners often undermined the arguments of other groups, such as the NUWSS, which were trying to move forwards using other methods. Emmeline and her supporters certainly got noticed, but members of the NUWSS were working hard at the same time to achieve change peacefully.

To raise money for the WSPU and her own campaigning work, Emmeline visited the United States. She gave speeches and lectures around the country, arguing that direct action was the only way to get noticed in Britain.

A newspaper reported her speech to a crowd in Buffalo, New York:

Now, you ask, is this worthwhile?... We think it is worthwhile. Some of us think it is worth dying for if it is going to give future generations for all time the right to govern themselves...
We want the co-operation of the best intellect of men with the best intellect of women, and it is just because we are women that we want our viewpoint considered in the government.

During the next general election in the United Kingdom, Emmeline organized a women's parliament and encouraged women to march to Downing Street, the prime minister's residence, with petitions demanding the vote. Thousands of women did this and they met with violent resistance from the police. Around a thousand women were arrested, often with force.

Over the next few years, Emmeline was arrested five times and put into prison four times. Her final stay in prison was for three years for the crime of "encouraging the women of Britain to rebel".

Like many other women imprisoned for taking direct action at this time, Emmeline refused to eat for periods of time while she was in prison. This was to draw the public's attention to the cause the women were fighting for.

In response to these hunger strikes, the government introduced the Cat and Mouse Act in 1913. This new law meant that women who went on hunger strike in prison would be released when they became very weak and close to death so they could go home to recover. This way, the government would not get bad publicity from having women dying for their cause in prison.

However, when the women had recovered their strength at home, they would be re-arrested and put back in prison to complete their sentence. Many people thought this law was very cruel.

When Emmeline was released following her own hunger strike in 1913 and became strong enough again, she travelled to the United States. She wanted to avoid being sent back to prison.

At first, she was held on Ellis Island in New York and was not allowed to travel any further, but many American campaigners complained about her treatment until President Woodrow Wilson ordered her release. She then went on to many meetings and lectures around the United States.

She made a very famous speech in Hartford, Connecticut in November that year. She explained why campaigners in the United Kingdom were resorting to desperate measures:

> This "Cat and Mouse Act" which is being used against women today has failed... There are women who are being carried from their sick beds on stretchers into meetings. They are too weak to speak, but they go amongst their fellow workers just to show that ... their spirit is alive.

Now, I want to say to you who think women cannot succeed, we have brought the government of England to this position, that it has to face this alternative: either women are to be killed or women are to have the vote... Well, there is only one answer... — you must give those women the vote.

When she returned to the United Kingdom, Emmeline was re-arrested. The next morning, women gathered in Westminster Abbey to pray aloud, chanting "God save Emmeline

Pankhurst!" When she was released from prison again, she travelled to Paris to recover.

World War I started in 1914 and, like many other campaigners, Emmeline shifted her energy to the war effort. She travelled to the United States, Canada and Russia, encouraging the employment of women in factories.

The important work done by women during the war could not be ignored and attitudes began to crumble in the face of the campaigners' arguments.

In 1918, the Representation of the People Act gave voting rights to British women over the age of 30. British women finally gained equal rights to men in 1928, giving them the right to vote at age 21. Emmeline died shortly afterwards, having finally won the right she had spent her life campaigning for.

Getting women into government

After women won the vote in the United States and the United Kingdom, the next step was to get women elected into government.

The first woman in the US Congress was Jeannette Rankin in 1917. Two years later, Nancy Astor became the first female Member of Parliament (MP) in the United Kingdom. Since those early days, almost 300 women have been elected in the United States and 369 British women have been elected as MPs.

However, there is still a long way to go. The percentage of women elected is still very small compared to men. There has only ever been one female British prime minister and the United States has yet to see its first female president.

Other important figures

Lucretia Mott (1793–1880)

Lucretia was a Quaker who campaigned to end slavery and for women's rights in the United States. Her husband founded the American Anti-Slavery Society and Lucretia was the first woman to speak at its meetings. Lucretia then set up the Philadelphia Female Anti-Slavery Society herself. She was barred from entering the World's Anti-Slavery Convention in 1840, where she met Elizabeth Cady Stanton and went on to help organize the Seneca Falls Convention. Lucretia was important in helping Elizabeth to organize the women's rights movement in the following years.

Alice Paul (1885–1977)

Alice was a women's rights activist in the United States. She also spent time in the United Kingdom, meeting the Pankhursts and other campaigners. She took direct action while living in London and was put in prison three times. On her return to the United States, Alice was involved in the first political protest outside the White House and was arrested and imprisoned as a result. She played a key role in the campaign that led to the 19th Amendment being passed in 1920, granting women the vote.

Millicent Fawcett (1847–1929)

Millicent was an early campaigner for women's right to vote in the United Kingdom. She worked hard to improve girls' education and helped to set up Newnham College in Cambridge. She became leader of the National Union of Women's Suffrage Societies in 1907 and held the post until 1919. Millicent did not believe in taking direct action to get results, but focused on gathering support for petitions and peaceful marches.

Annie Kenney (1879–1953)

Annie was born into a poor, working-class family in Yorkshire. She began work in a cotton mill when she was only 10 years old but still managed to go to school. When she heard Christabel Pankhurst speaking about women's rights in 1905, she joined the Women's Social and Political Union (WSPU). She was arrested later that year after shouting a question out at a political meeting and receiving no answer. Annie became deputy leader of the WSPU in 1912 and went on hunger strike while in prison. During World War I, she travelled around the United Kingdom, encouraging trade unions to support the war effort.

Emily Davison (1872–1913)

Emily Davison was born in London in 1872. She was well-educated and studied at Oxford University before becoming a teacher. She believed in taking direct action to win greater rights for women and she joined the WSPU in 1906. Emily was a very active member of the organization and was often arrested. She was imprisoned in Manchester in 1909, when the authorities tried to force-feed her. Emily is remembered because she ran in front of the king's horse as it took part in a race. She may have just wanted to gain attention for the fight for women's right to vote, but she was trampled by the horse and died.

Timeline

1815   Elizabeth Cady Stanton is born.

1820   Susan B. Anthony is born.

1840   Elizabeth Cady Stanton and Lucretia Mott are stopped from entering the World's Anti-Slavery Convention in London.

1848   First women's rights convention is held in Seneca Falls, New York.

1853   Clementina Black is born.

1858   Emmeline Pankhurst is born.

1859   Carrie Chapman Catt is born.

1867   14th Amendment passes Congress. For the first time, the US Constitution describes a citizen as "male". Susan B. Anthony forms the Equal Rights Association.

1869 National Woman Suffrage Association is founded with Elizabeth Cady Stanton as president. American Woman Suffrage Association (AWSA) is formed. Wyoming gives women the vote.

1870 Married Women's Property Act in the United Kingdom allows women to own their own property.

1888 Clementina Black gets first successful equal pay resolution.

1890 The National Woman Suffrage Association (NWSA) and AWSA join together to form the National American Woman Suffrage Association (NAWSA) in the United States.

1893 New Zealand becomes the first country where women can vote. Colorado votes to give women suffrage.

1897 National Union of Women's Suffrage Societies (NUWSS) starts in the UK.

1903 The Pankhursts form the Women's Social and Political Union (WSPU) in the UK.

1905 Christabel Pankhurst and Annie Kenney are imprisoned after disrupting an election rally.

1907 Millicent Fawcett becomes leader of the NUWSS.

1908 250,000 people gather in Hyde Park, London to support the vote for women.

1910 Women in the US start to use parades, pickets and rallies to gain support. Women in Washington state gain the vote.

1912 Annie Kenney becomes leader of the WSPU.

1913 The Cat and Mouse Act is enacted: the government can temporarily release women from prison if they are on hunger strike and imprison them again once fit.

Rally is held in Hyde Park for women's right to vote.

1914 The start of World War I means women do more jobs that only men had done previously.

1917 Jeannette Rankin is elected to the US Congress.

1918 World War I ends and women in the UK over the age of 30 are allowed to vote.

1919 Nancy Astor is elected Member of Parliament in Britain.

1920 Women in the United States win the right to vote.

1928 Women in the United Kingdom over the age of 21 are able to vote.

Find out more

Books

Bring Out the Banners, Geoffrey Trease (A&C Black, 2013)

Elizabeth Cady Stanton and Susan B. Anthony: A Friendship That Changed the World, Penny Colman (Christy Ottaviano Books, 2011)

Rightfully Ours: How Women Won the Vote, Kerrie Logan Hollihan (Ball Publishing, 2012)

Suffragette (My Story), Carol Drinkwater (Scholastic, 2011)

Websites

www.bbc.co.uk/archive/suffragettes

Listen to fascinating recordings of women who were involved in the fight for the vote in Britain on this BBC website.

www.elizabethcadystanton.org

Find out more about Elizabeth Cady Stanton on this website.

www.nationalarchives.gov.uk/ education/focuson/film/film-archive/ archive.asp?catID=2&subCatID=2

You can watch film clips of rallies for women's suffrage in the United Kingdom on this website.

www.nwhm.org

Find out more about campaigners for women's rights in the United States on the National Women's History Museum website.

Glossary

abolitionist person who fought to end slavery

activist person who believes strongly in political or social change and takes part in activities such as public protests to try to make this happen

amendment making a change to something, usually a document, to improve it

boycott refusing to buy or use something in order to apply political pressure

campaigner person who works to raise other people's awareness of an issue

congressman member of the United States Congress, the part of the United States government that makes laws

convention large meeting of people who come to a place, usually for several days, to talk about their shared work or other interests or to make decisions as a group

custody officially in care of children

delegate person who goes to a meeting and represents others

direct action activities in public that protest against something

domestic to do with the home and family

legislature governing body that makes laws and can also amend or repeal them

minimum wage lowest wage allowed to be paid to someone

mobilize get people together to do something

petition written request for change, signed by many people

Quaker member of a Christian group also known as the Society of Friends, which supports peace and is against war

radical person wanting to make extreme changes

rally big meeting

registrar person whose job is to record births, deaths and marriages

suffrage right to vote

temperance avoiding alcohol

trade union organized group of workers who support each other's rights and interests

Index

National Union of Women's Suffrage Societies (NUWSS) 84, 86–87, 99
National Woman Suffrage Association (NWSA) 24, 39, 41, 42–43
New York State Woman's Rights Committee 33
New Zealand 43

Pankhurst, Adela 85
Pankhurst, Christabel 80, 85, 100
Pankhurst, Emmeline 76–92
Pankhurst, Richard 79, 80, 83
Pankhurst, Sylvia 80, 85
Paul, Alice 71, 98
peace activism 75
peaceful protest 77, 84, 87, 99
Philadelphia Female Anti-Slavery Society 97
politicians, female 95
Post, Amy 29
poverty 29, 48, 49–50, 59, 81–82
property rights 5, 8, 14, 16, 34, 79
public speaking 18, 20, 64, 68, 72, 74, 87, 90–91

Quakers 27, 97

Rankin, Jeanette 95
Revolution, The 23, 38

Seneca Falls Convention 7, 14–15, 29
slavery 10, 21, 22–23, 28, 36–37
Stanton, Elizabeth Cady 6–25, 30–32, 33, 38, 39, 43, 79, 97
Stanton, Henry 10–11, 12
strikes 51, 53
suffrage 22–23, 24, 32–33, 37–43, 59–60, 64, 66–75, 77–92, 97–101
Suffrage Declaration 59
suffragettes 86
sweatshops 57

temperance movement 29–30, 32
trade unions 50, 100
Trades Union Congress 50–51

USA 6–43, 62–75, 95, 97–98

war work 21, 61, 92
wedding vows 10–11
Wilson, Woodrow 73, 90

Women's Franchise Declaration Committee 59–60
Women's Franchise League 80
Women's Industrial Council (WIC) 55
Women's Loyal National League 22
Women's New York State Temperance Society 32
Women's Protective and Provident League (WPPL) 48, 49
Women's Social and Political Union (WSPU) 77, 84–85, 86, 87, 100, 101
Women's Trade Union Association 54–55
Women's Trade Union League 49
workhouses 81–82
working women 48–49, 50–55, 56–59, 60–61
World War I 60–61, 75, 92, 100
World's Anti-Slavery Convention 11, 97